WHY DO I
BLEED?

BY KIRSTY HOLMES

CRABTREE
PUBLISHING COMPANY
WWW.CRABTREEBOOKS.COM

Published in Canada
Crabtree Publishing
616 Welland Avenue
St. Catharines, ON
L2M 5V6

Published in the United States
Crabtree Publishing
PMB 59051
350 Fifth Ave, 59th Floor
New York, NY 10118

Published in 2019 by Crabtree Publishing Company

First Published by Book Life in 2018
Copyright © 2018 Book Life

Printed in the U.S.A./082018/CG20180601

Author: Kirsty Holmes

Editors: Madeline Tyler, Kathy Middleton

Design: Danielle Rippengill

Proofreader: Janine Deschenes

Prepress technician: Samara Parent

Print coordinator: Katharine Berti

All facts, statistics, web addresses and URLs in this book were verified as valid and accurate at time of writing. No responsibility for any changes to external websites or references can be accepted by either the author or publisher.

Photographs

All images are courtesy of Shutterstock.com, unless otherwise specified. With thanks to Getty Images, Thinkstock Photo and iStockphoto. Front Cover & 1 – Dmitry Natashin, Nadzin, Jemastock, hvostik. Images used on every spread – Nadzin, TheFarAwayKingdom. 2 – johavel, anpanna 4 – emastock, hvostik. 5 – Iconic Bestiary. 6 & 7 – johavel, anpannan, VasutinSergey. 8 & 9 – Andy Frith. 10 & 11 – LOVE YOU, VasutinSergey. 12 & 13 – Creative Mood. 14 & 15 – vladwel, Elena Paletskaya. 16 – DRogatnev, Nadia Buravleva. 17 – svtdesign. 18 – naulicreative, johavel, anpannan. 19 – gritsalak karalak. 20 – Photoroyalty. 21 – Lexamer. 22 – vladwel, Nadya_Ar. 23 – johavel, anpannan, wectors.

Library and Archives Canada Cataloguing in Publication

Holmes, Kirsty Louise, author
       Why do I bleed? / Kirsty Holmes.

(Why do I?)
Includes index.
Issued in print and electronic formats.
ISBN 978-0-7787-5133-5 (hardcover).--
ISBN 978-0-7787-5146-5 (softcover).--
ISBN 978-1-4271-2170-7 (HTML)

       1. Blood--Juvenile literature. 2. Blood--Circulation--Juvenile literature.
3. Cardiovascular system--Juvenile literature. 4. Human physiology--Juvenile
literature. I. Title.

QP91.H65 2018   j612.1'1   C2018-902394-5
                                         C2018-902395-3

Library of Congress Cataloging-in-Publication Data

Names: Holmes, Kirsty, author.
Title: Why do I bleed? / Kirsty Holmes.
Description: New York, New York : Crabtree Publishing Company, 2019. |
   Series: Why do I? | Includes index.
Identifiers: LCCN 2018021329 (print) | LCCN 2018021635 (ebook) |
   ISBN 9781427121707 (Electronic) |
   ISBN 9780778751335 (hardcover) |
   ISBN 9780778751465 (pbk.)
Subjects: LCSH: Blood--Juvenile literature. | Cardiovascular system--Juvenile
   literature. | Human physiology--Juvenile literature.
Classification: LCC QP91 (ebook) | LCC QP91 .H694 2019 (print) |
   DDC 612.1/1--dc23
LC record available at https://lccn.loc.gov/2018021329

CONTENTS

Words that look like **this** can be found in the glossary on page 24.

Do You Need a Bandage?

Have you ever cut your finger, had a bloody nose, or needed a bandage for your knee?

What is that red stuff in your body, and what does it do?

When you cut or scratch your skin, the red stuff that comes out is your blood. Blood is very important—and it's supposed to stay inside you!

But what exactly is blood? Where does it come from?

5

What Is Blood For?

All humans and most animals have blood inside their bodies. We need it to live. Blood has a lot of really important jobs to do.

REALLY GOOD STUFF

Blood travels all through our bodies. It carries useful things, such as **oxygen**, to the body parts that need them. Blood also heals cuts and helps protect us from illnesses. But how?

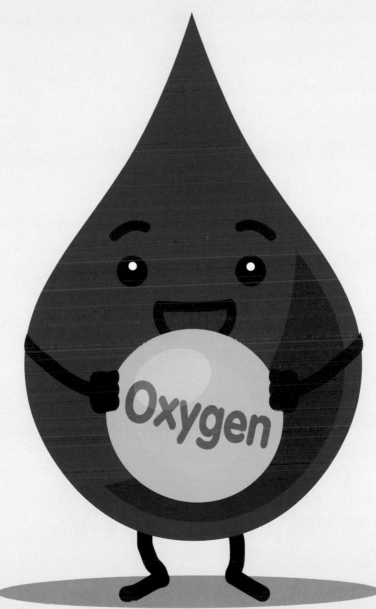

Red or White?

What is in your blood?

Blood is made up of tiny parts called cells. Red blood cells carry oxygen around the body.

White blood cells attack and destroy diseases and germs.

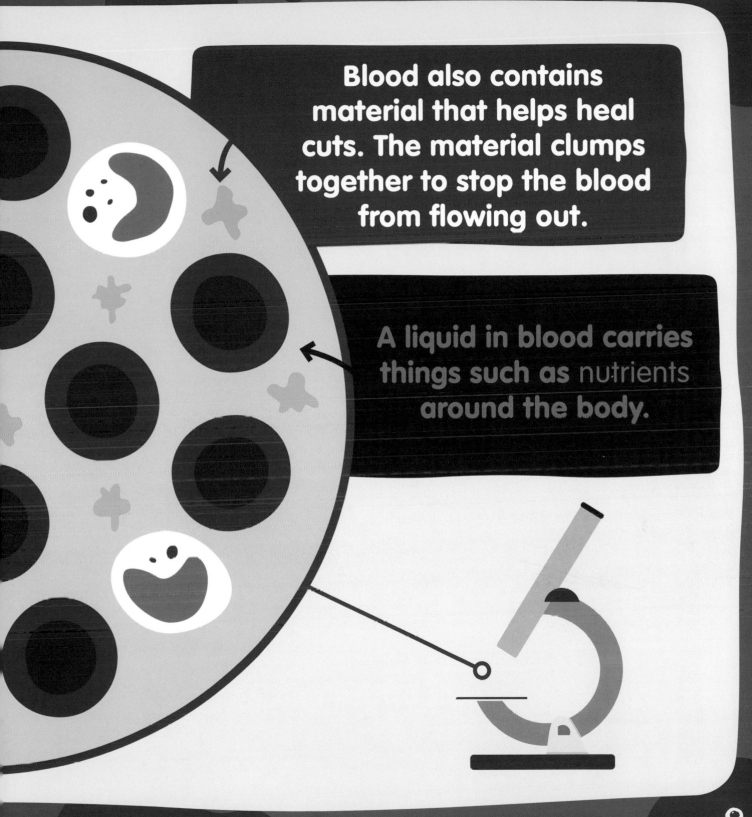

Blood also contains material that helps heal cuts. The material clumps together to stop the blood from flowing out.

A liquid in blood carries things such as nutrients around the body.

The Heart Pumps Blood

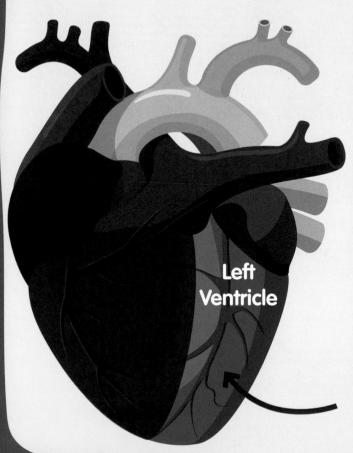

Left Ventricle

Your heart is an organ. An organ is a body part that does a job.

The heart's job is to pump your blood around your body.

The left side of your heart is called the left ventricle. It sends blood full of oxygen from the lungs to the rest of the body.

The right side of the heart is called the right ventricle. It sends the used blood back to the lungs to be filled with oxygen again.

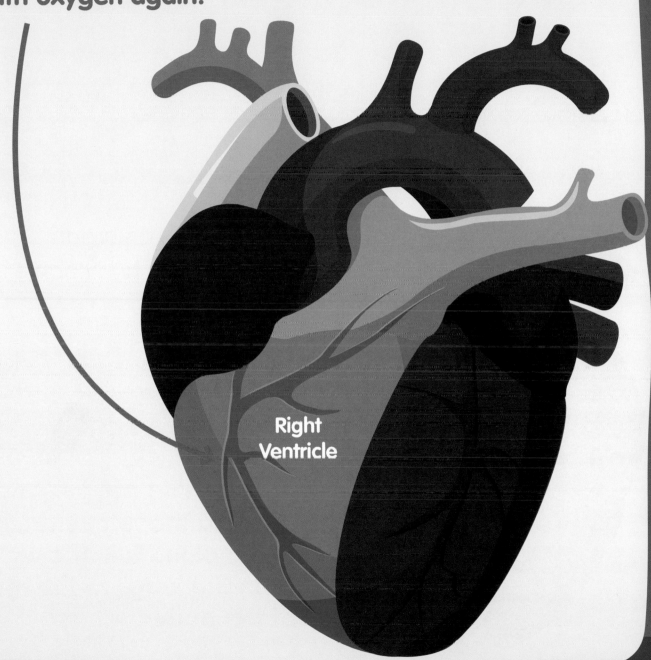

Right
Ventricle

Feel the Beat

As your heart pumps the blood, it beats in a steady rhythm. If you listen to someone's chest, you will hear a bump-bump, bump-bump sound. This is called a heartbeat.

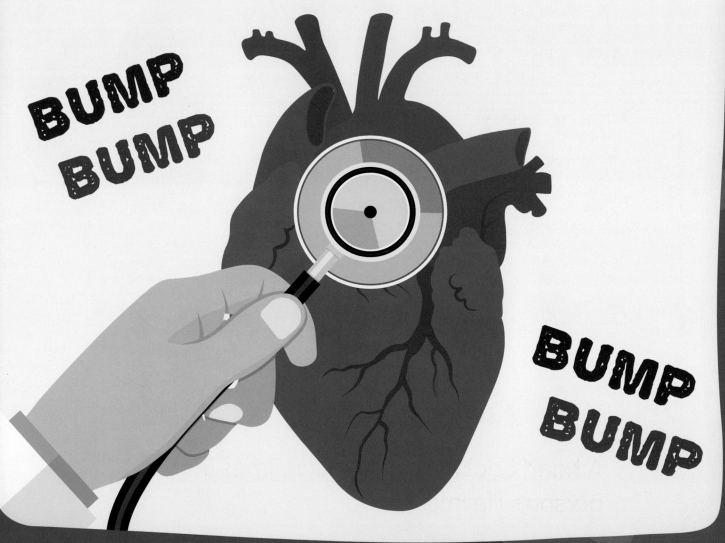

BUMP BUMP

BUMP BUMP

A heart beats over 2.5 billion times in a person's lifetime!

Veins and Arteries

The tubes that move blood from the heart around the body are called blood vessels. There are two types of vessels.

Veins are vessels that carry used blood back to the heart.

Arteries are vessels that carry blood with oxygen away from the heart.

Squeeze your hand to make a tight fist. Look at your wrist. You should be able to see your veins and arteries at work!

Blood Gets Around

Blood is circulated, which means it is moved throughout our bodies.

STEP 1:
You breathe in oxygen through your nose and mouth. The oxygen travels to your lungs.

You couldn't live without blood! Follow the oxygen around this body and see where it goes.

Oxygen

Oxygen

Oxygen

Oxygen

Oxygen

STEP 3:

Your arteries are tubes that carry blood filled with oxygen.

Heart

Lungs

Artery

Vein

STEP 2:

Oxygen in the lungs enters the blood. Your heart beats like a pump to push the blood around your body.

STEP 4:

When the oxygen in the blood gets used up, tubes called veins carry the blood back to the heart. The blood gets pumped to the lungs to be filled with oxygen again.

Scabs and Scratches

Blood belongs inside your body. If you cut yourself or have a nosebleed, your blood will flow outside of your body.

RED ALERT!

RED ALERT!

Blood on the outside of your body could be a sign that something is wrong.

18

A special material in your blood quickly fills up any cut on your body. It stops the bleeding by forming a hard crust on top of the cut, called a scab.

Never pick a scab. It will fall off by itself when your skin has healed.

Know Your Type

A B AB O

There are different types of blood. Blood type is based on the kind of red blood cells you have. You can be type A, B, AB, or O.

If a person has an accident and loses a lot of blood, they can be given blood from another person. A person who gives blood to another person is called a **donor**.

A donor's blood type must match the blood type of the person receiving the blood.

Do you know what your blood type is?

Blood Busters!

If all your blood vessels were laid in a straight line, it would be over 60,000 miles (almost 100,000 km) long!

A blue whale has the largest heart of any living thing.

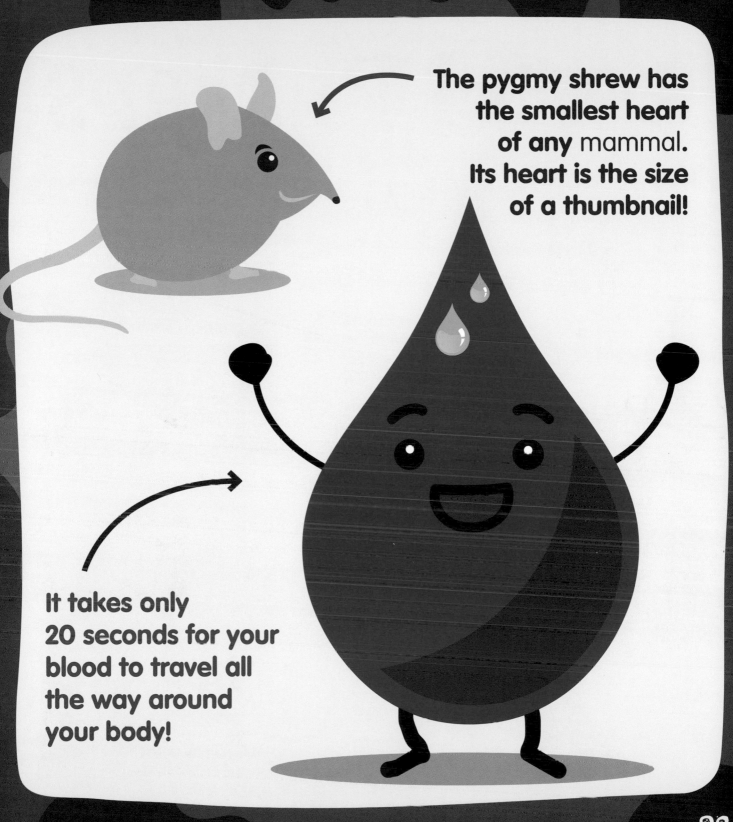

The pygmy shrew has the smallest heart of any mammal. Its heart is the size of a thumbnail!

It takes only 20 seconds for your blood to travel all the way around your body!

Glossary

cells   The tiny parts that make up every living thing

donor   A person who donates their healthy blood, organs, or other body parts to help others who need them

germs   Tiny living things that cause disease, or make us sick

mammals   Animals that grow hair, have warm blood and a backbone, and produce milk to feed their babies

nutrients   Substances that people need to grow and stay healthy

oxygen   A natural gas that all living things need to survive

Index